RESOURCE GUIDE for Where in the World is the MOON?

Written by Molly Davis
Illustrated by Carrie Lacey Boerio

Developed and compiled by Denise V. Carskadon and Anne C. Albrecht

RESOURCE GUIDE for *Where in the World is the Moon?*
Copyright © 2021 Mary C. Davis, Readitagain LLC, Columbus, Ohio

All rights reserved.
Library of Congress Control Number 2021921616
ISBN 9780578306094
Printed in the United States of America

ENGLISH LANGUAGE ARTS (ELA)

Vocabulary of words not in the book

Eight phases of the moon.

We cannot see the new moon.

We can see all other moon phases.

1. New moon, dark, we cannot see
2. Waxing crescent, starts skinny and seems grow bigger on left side
3. First-quarter moon, half-moon bright on its right side
4. Waxing gibbous, bigger than half-moon on left side, not as big as full moon
5. Full moon, big circle
6. Waning gibbous, getting smaller than full moon, smaller on right side
7. Last-quarter moon, a half-moon bright on left side
8. Waning crescent, getting skinnier, smaller on the right side

RESOURCE GUIDE
for *Where in the World is the Moon?*

Developed and compiled by
Denise V. Carskadon and Anne C. Albrecht

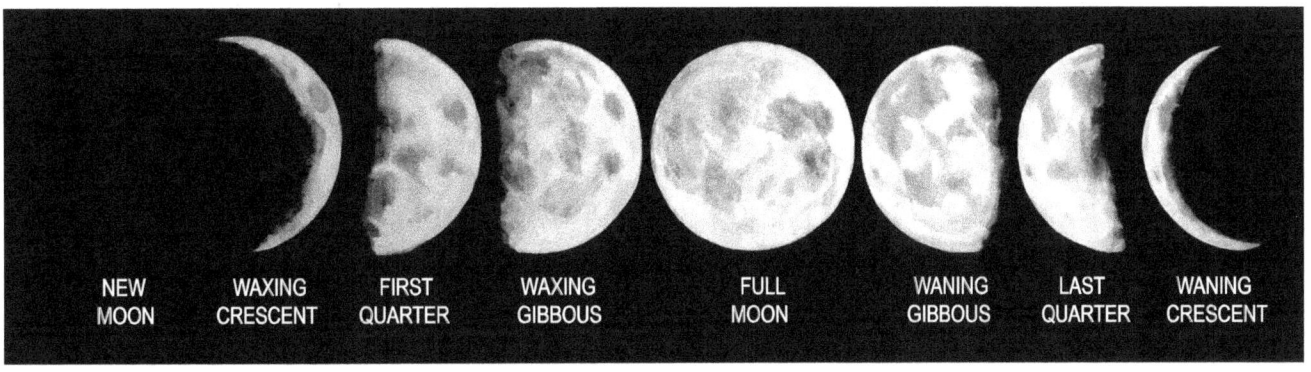

This resource guide, developed to supplement *Where in the World is the Moon?* by Molly Davis, is also a learning tool for any other children's book about Earth's moon. We developed and compiled the guide to support teachers, librarians, homeschoolers, and parents of students in kindergarten through second grade.

The guide offers ideas and activities to integrate *Where in the World is the Moon?* or other children's books about Earth's moon into English language arts (ELA), science, and related arts curricula.

ENGLISH LANGUAGE ARTS (ELA)

Cause and effect
Cause is the reason something happened (e.g., the moon's gravity)

Effect is the result of what happened (e.g., the tides happening in the oceans)

www.teacherspayteachers.com foldable flip books and interactive templates.

Journaling
Keep a moon notebook for one month, starting with the new moon.

Note what days you can see the moon and what time you saw it.

Draw what it looked like.

Similes and metaphors – divide into similes or metaphors:
Great big smile

Faint as a feather

Sliver-curved arm bent with its elbow sticking out

Bright grand self

Moon peek

Tippytoed above the horizon

ENGLISH LANGUAGE ARTS (ELA)

Think of a question that is answered in the book.
    Is the moon out only at night?
    Does the moon change shape?

Vocabulary of words in *Where in the World is the Moon?*
    Bent – Curved, or not straight
    Fade – To lose brightness or color
    Faint – Barely noticeable
    Horizon – The line where the earth and sky appear to meet
    Pale – Having little color
    Scoots – Moves along, usually quickly
    Sliver – A small, thin piece of something cut or split from a larger piece
    Strewn – Something that is spread out in a scattered way

ENGLISH LANGUAGE ARTS (ELA)

Vocabulary words not in the book

Craters – Big, bowl-shaped pits on the moon

Gravity – A force that brings things towards the center of the earth

Half-moon – When half of the near side of the moon's surface is lit

Orbit – Moon's circular path around Earth

Phases – Half of the moon is always sunlit. Phases are the different aspects of the moon's lit parts that we can see, except for first phase, the new moon, which we cannot see.

Sphere – A ball

Tide – The rising and falling of the sea

Books: Fiction

Moonstruck-Poems About Our Moon, edited by Rogers Stevens (Grades 2-5)

Isdahl, Nansubago Nagada. *Sing to the Moon*

Pfister, Marcus. *Sun and Moon* (Grades 1-2)

ENGLISH LANGUAGE ARTS (ELA)

Books: Non-Fiction

Beaton, Kathryn. *Tell Me Why the Moon Changes Shape* (Grades 1-3)
Berger, Melvin and Gilda. *The Moon* (Grades K-2)
Black, Vanessa. *Space Voyager-Moon* (Grades 1-2)
Branley, Franklyn M. *The Moon Seems to Change* (grades 2-3) (K-4)
Branley, Franklyn M. *What the Moon is Like* (Grades 1-4)
Cole, Joanna. *The Magic School Bus Takes a Moonwalk* (GradesK-3)
Cowan, Laura. *The Usborne Book of the Moon* (Grades Pre-K)
Crane, Cody, *The Moon* (Grades K-2)
DeCristofano, Carolyn Hinami. *The Sun and the Moon* (Grades K-2)
Gibbons, Gail, *The Moon Book* (Grades K-3)
Hansen, Grace. *The Moon* (Grades PK-2)
Harman, Alice *Moon (Fact Finders)* (Grades 2-3)
Lassieur, Allison. *The Moon* (Grades K-2)
Morgan, Emily. *Next Time You See the Moon*
Simon, Seymour. *The Moon* (Grades 2-5)
Sommer, Nathan. *Space Science, The Moon*
Tomecek, Steve. *Our Universe: The Moon*
Turnbull, Stephanie. *Sun, Moon, and Stars* (Grades K-2)
Waxman, Laura Hamilton. *The Moon* (Grades 1-3)
Ziefert, Harriet. *You Can't Ride a Bicycle to the Moon* (Grades 2-5)

SCIENCE

K—W—L Chart
Create a K-W-L chart with the kids about the moon.

What I **KNOW** about the moon	What I **WANT TO KNOW** about the moon	What I **LEARNED** about the moon

Chart of the moon phases:

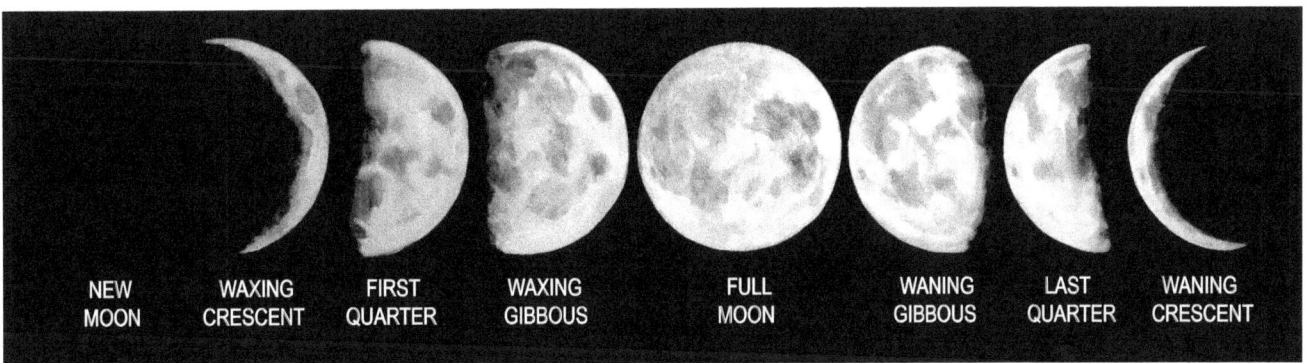

SCIENCE

Create a Venn Diagram using sun and moon facts.

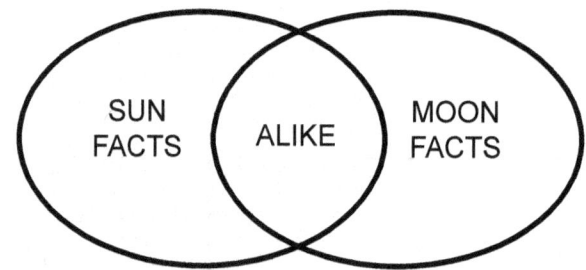

Sun facts
- Source of light and heat.
- Rises, morning. Sets, evening.
- We only see in the day.
- Looks the same every day.

Moon facts
- Not a source of light or heat. It reflects the sun's light.
- Rises and sets at various times of the day and night.
- We sometimes see night or day.
- Looks different from time to time throughout the month.

Sun and moon facts
- Sun and moon are spheres.
- Sun and moon rise in the east.
- Sun and moon set in the west.

SCIENCE

Sort these statements into a facts and myths

The moon has no light of its own.
The moon reflects light from the sun.
The moon changes its shape.
There is a dark side of the moon.
The cow jumped over the moon.
The moon is made of Swiss cheese.
There is a man's face in the moon.

Facts	Myths

Directions — Compass

Words used: Eastern and west

Teachers could integrate directions and use of the compass with a unit on Earth's moon.

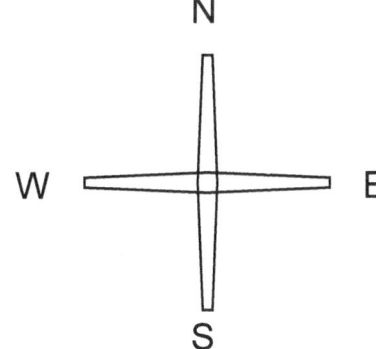

SCIENCE

Interactive experiments

Flashlight, ball, etc. to show moon's phases:
https://www.youtube.com/watch?v=wz01pTvuMa0

Make moon craters with flour and marbles and golf balls.

Make moon sand with eight cups of flour and one cup of baby oil.

Curve your fingers and thumb on your right hand. When the moon looks like this, it is waxing or growing.

Curve the fingers and thumb on your left hand. When the moon looks like this, it is waning or shrinking.

GOOD SCIENCE CURRICULUM WEBSITES:

https://www.nasa.gov/kidsclub/index.html
(great ideas for crafts, activities, eBooks)

www.amyswandering.com
Free homeschool science curriculum

RELATED ARTS

Art projects, interactive

Using eight Oreo cookies, cut the cream parts into moon shapes to show moon phases.

Draw a chart of moon phases.

Make moon phase cards.

Movement

To demonstrate how the moon moves around the earth, kids can form a circle.

One child represents the sun on the outside of the circle; one child represents Earth in the center of the circle; and eight kids, each one represents one of the moon's phases.

Each child could have a large poster board and create artwork of the role being played.

FREE AND PRINTABLE GRAPHIC ORGANIZERS

www.studenthandouts.com

www.Homeschoolgivewaways.com

www.easyteacherworksheets.com

www.Hmhco.com (Houghton, Mifflin, Harcourt)

www.Pinterest.com (search for free graphic organizers)

www.teacherspayteachers.com — interactive notebook templates

www.teacherspayteachers.com/Store/Digital-Mojo — clipart flaps

www.teacherkarma.com — foldable flip books and interactive templates

YOUTUBE VIDEOS TO SUPPORT LEARNING
As of August 1, 2021, we found these excellent YouTube sites:

Song
"Time to Shine" by Storybots
https://youtu.be/i235Y2HRksA

YOUTUBE VIDEOS TO SUPPORT LEARNING *continued*

Phases of the Moon | Learn All About the Moon for Kids!
https://www.youtube.com/watch?v=kFR7HLRMx_o

Moon's Phases
https://www.youtube.com/watch?v=1sj2otIjZfM

Morgan, Emily, Next Time You See the Moon
https://www.youtube.com/watch?v=wz01pTvuMa0

Oreo as moon phases
https://www.youtube.com/watch?v=tqDiE2P7qJ8 (two videos)
https://www.youtube.com/watch?v=Az5x8d5ZX5k

Nadia's Books, Branley, Franklyn, The Moon Seems to Change
https://www.youtube.com/watch?v=aJ1y8Gr4FcQ

Celestial Storytime reads: Branley, Frankyn, What the Moon is Like
https://www.youtube.com/watch?v=vVepPRFHjmo

Free School, Phases of the Moon: Astronomy and Space for Kids
https://www.youtube.com/watch?v=JM21GBJecx0

Turtle Diary: Phases of the Moon | Science Videos for Kids
https://www.youtube.com/watch?v=t6MCtB752AE

Tata Storytime: Isdahl, Nansugaga Nagada. Sing to the Moon
https://www.youtube.com/watch?v=krzDl_2b4bs

ReadingLibraryBooks, Bo Hyeon Seo, What Shape is the Moon?
https://www.youtube.com/watch?v=9trCBIHQT6I

NOTES

NOTES

www.ingramcontent.com/pod-product-compliance
Lightning Source LLC
Chambersburg PA
CBHW051216290426
44109CB00021B/2476